Mushrooms:

20 Simple to Advanced Techniques How To Grow Mushrooms At Home

The information herein is offered for informational purposes solely, and is universal as so. The presentation of the information is without contract or any type of guarantee assurance.

The trademarks that are used are without any consent, and the publication of the trademark is without permission or backing by the trademark owner. All trademarks and brands within this book are for clarifying purposes only and are the owned by the owners themselves, not affiliated with this document.

Table of content

Introduction

It is highly likely that you already consume the standard white mushrooms which are found in virtually every supermarket around the world. However, there is a huge range of options when it comes to mushrooms. Many people spend years studying different types in order to be able to identify them and pick them in the wild. Of course, this is not an option for anyone who is uncertain of the difference between two mushrooms which look almost the same but one of which will make you extremely ill whilst the other is good to eat!

The risks involved with attempting to recognize different species of mushrooms and the time involved in locating these mushrooms in the wild means that this is not an option for many people. There are ten main types of mushrooms that can easily be identified and added to your food and transform the flavor of your cooking. Whilst the common button mushroom is an excellent choice for some dishes, there are arrange of opportunities when you will find that one of the other types of mushrooms can provide an even better flavor:

Chanterelles

These golden colored mushrooms group together and look like a large flower. They actually have a fruity taste with a hint of pepper. Surprisingly delicate they can make a good accompaniment to any egg dish.

Cremini

These mushrooms are very similar to the traditional white button mushroom. In effect they are a more mature version of the white button. They will usually be a similar shape and size but will be a light brown color instead of white. Their flavor is slightly stronger than the white button mushroom but is still mild enough to include in all your favorite dishes.

Morel

This type of mushroom is often referred to as a dead honeycomb and is a dark brown in color. Despite its looks it is incredibly tasty and can be added to almost any recipe as a lively substitute to the standard mushroom.

Portobello

This is another one that you have probably already heard of. It is actually a whit button mushroom in its final stages of maturity. The cap is fully grown and spreads out over the stalk. It is often used to replace meat in dishes as it has the same texture. It is also mild and can be delicious simply grilled.

Enoki

The first time you see these you may think you are looking at a bean sprout. They have very long stems and tiny little heads. As opposed to many mushrooms they are crisp and can make an excellent addition to a salad as well as soups.

Shiitake

These mushrooms have been used in Asian cooking for many years as this is
where the mushroom originates from. However, it is possible to grow it in other
climates. They have a meaty flavor and are often used on top of dishes or to improve the flavor of a sauce or even soup. It is also possible to purchase them in
powder form.

Oyster

These layered white creations look nothing like the common button mushroom
but they are delicious with a slightly sweet flavor. They are very easy to grow and
are often found in the wild.

Button

These need no introduction as you will have, undoubtedly, already used them
regularly in your cooking. As a young mushroom they tend to have an earthy flavor.

Porcini

This mushroom has a delicious meaty flavor with a hint of nuts! It is light brown
and can be as small as one inch or even ten inches in size. It is a regular addition
to Italian cooking.

Hen of the Woods

These are often found at the bottom of dying oak trees or any other hardwood
tree which is in the last moments of its life. They cluster together and can look
like a hen from a distance, (hence the name). This type of mushroom is often

used by the Japanese, as well as the western world, and they have a rich, earthy flavor.

 There are many other types of mushrooms but these are the ones which are most likely to pleasure your palette and can be fairly easily grown at home.

Chapter 1 – Tools & Equipment Needed to Grow Mushrooms at Home

Growing mushrooms at home is a fairly simple process, once you know what you are doing. However, as is the case with most jobs, having the right tools can make a big difference to your success. It is best to work out which type or types of mushroom you intend to grow. This will ensure you have the opportunity to research if they need anything in particular and acquire the right equipment before you start growing them.

The following items are easy to find but will be exceptionally beneficial when you start to grow your own mushrooms:

The mushrooms!

http://www.mushrooms.ca/images/mushroom-group.png

In order to grow mushrooms you need to have some of their seeds. These are generally referred to as spores. They are usually very small and can be purchased from many garden supplies stores. Once you have grown your own mushrooms it is possible to collect spores from your own mushrooms to use in future years.

Pressure Cooker Jars

An alternative to this is simply jam jars with good, sealable lids. This is for the mushrooms to grow in without being exposed to other contaminants which could affect their growth or quality.

The Substrate

This is the substances you will place in the bottom of the jars for the spores to start growing in. It is different depending upon the types of mushrooms you are attempting to grow although straw is generally a good substrate for a wide variety of types.

Additional Bits

There is a whole range of other bits which will prove to be useful during the process of growing mushrooms; these include a knife, spray bottle, syringes, gloves, a mouth mask, Petri dish, disinfectants and a thermometer.

Once you have acquired all these pieces of equipment you will be ready to start growing mushrooms:

Stage 1

The most obvious starting point is to find a location where you will be able to grow your mushrooms. This may be in your shed, green house or even in the house. The important thing to remember is that mushrooms generally like to grow in damp places which are cool and preferably dark. If this in your house you may have a basement, or you may be happy to keep them in one of your cup-boards. A shelve out of direct sunlight will be fine in your shed whilst a specific enclosure will be needed if you are intending to attempt to grown them in the greenhouse. It is worth noting that the air in the green house will probably be too warm and dry for your mushrooms.

http://inspectapedia.com/sickhouse/MushroomsIndoors010DJF.jpg

It is best to test the location you have chosen by using your thermometer and checking the temperature throughout the day. In general you will need the temperature to stay between fifty and sixty degrees Fahrenheit. The more advanced mushroom growing requires the use of more natural conditions, such as rotting logs and should be something that you move onto.

Once you have chosen your spot you can start growing! The spores will need to be sprinkled onto the substrate. You will need to choose the substrate according to what kind of mushrooms you intend to grow. You can use baking trays although the Petri dishes are the easiest option as you can monitor the progress of the spores. The Petri dishes should be kept at a temperature of approximately seventy degrees Fahrenheit. You may find it easiest to do this by resting them on a heat pad. After about three weeks you should start to see the tiny roots on the spores. These are very small and appear like delicate threads. At this point you will need to remove them from the heat and put them where the temperature is in the fifty to sixty range. You should also cover each dish with a thin layer of soil.

Each dish will need covering with a damp cloth. The cloth can be kept damp by spraying it regularly with water in your spray bottle. You should avoid letting the cloth dry out.

Tip 1

http://www.rodalesor-ganiclife.com/sites/rodalesorganiclife.com/files/articles/2015/04/shiitake3-1100.jpg

As a point of reference it is useful to note that button mushrooms, Shiitake and oyster are the easiest ones to grow at home. As such these are the best ones for you to start your mushroom growing experience with.

Tip 2

Each of these mushrooms has their own preferred substrates. Button mushrooms grow best in a bed of composted manure, whilst oyster mushrooms prefer straw. Shiitakes are different again; their preferred medium is hardwood sawdust. It is possible to use straw or sawdust for all of these mushrooms but the best results will be had when you use their preferred substrate.

https://mushroomrec.files.wordpress.com/2013/11/mush-spore.gif

It is best to locate good quality spores not spawn. Although it is possible to mushrooms from spawn, in fact it is generally easier. It is more satisfying and the mushrooms generally taste better when grown from the spores and you control every step of the process. Spawn is straw or an equivalent substrate which has already had spores spread over it and they have started to grow. Providing you handle the spawn correctly it will grow into edible mushrooms in a relatively short space of time. The advantage of spawn is that it is already visible whereas most spores are not visible to the naked human eye.

Stage 2

Having successfully planted the mushroom spores the next most important part is monitoring the progress. Ideally you should monitor the temperature daily to ensure it stays within the desired range. If it starts to get too warm you may need to consider moving the growing mushrooms. Alternatively too cool may required a small heat source; but you do not want to overheat them!

At the same time as you monitor the temperature, you should be checking that the cloth is still damp and squirting it with additional water if necessary. The cloth should never be saturated as this will be too much water for the mushrooms and is likely to damage if not kill them.

This process should take approximately three weeks, at the end of which you will start to see small mushrooms appearing. These are the beginnings of your very own edible mushrooms.

Stage 3

You will need to continue monitoring the temperature and the moisture level as the mushroom continue to grow. The growth is surprisingly quick now that they are becoming established.

Usually within two weeks the mushroom will be fully grown and the cap will move away from the stalk to form a distinct shape, separate to the stalk. This is the sign that they are ready to pick and eat.

Tip 4

http://media.treehugger.com/assets/images/2011/10/mushroom-magic.jpg

It should be possible to grip the mushroom between your finger and thumb and pull. This is an effective way of picking mushrooms, however, this is also likely to damage the fungi which has only recently developed; this is the foundation of the mushrooms and will allow future mushrooms to grow. It is therefore advisable not to pluck the mushrooms; instead use you scalpel or knife to cut the bottom of their stalk. The fungi will not be damaged and you will have additional mushrooms in the future!

Tip 5

It is best to wash your mushrooms before eating them. Although they have been grown in a controlled environment you can never be too certain where there may be dangerous substances. They may have attached themselves to the mushrooms whilst they were growing or may even have been in the substrate already. Washing ensures they are clean. You can then store them in a paper bag for up to one week. After this they will lose their color and start to soften. They will no longer taste as nice and may even start to go bad. It is important to remember that a mushroom is simply a form of fungi. Whilst they are very enjoyable, if you eat them once they go bad they can make you ill.

Chapter 2 – Five Tips for The Right Start to Your Mushroom Growing Project

Although in essence growing mushrooms is straight forward there are a variety of issues which can be resolved and help to make your mushrooms taste better, grow better and improve the overall experience. It is also worth noting that a good crop of mushrooms can be harvested everyday and provide you with mushrooms for as long as six months. This will provide you with plenty of opportunities to show off your green fingers to friends and family.

Tip 1

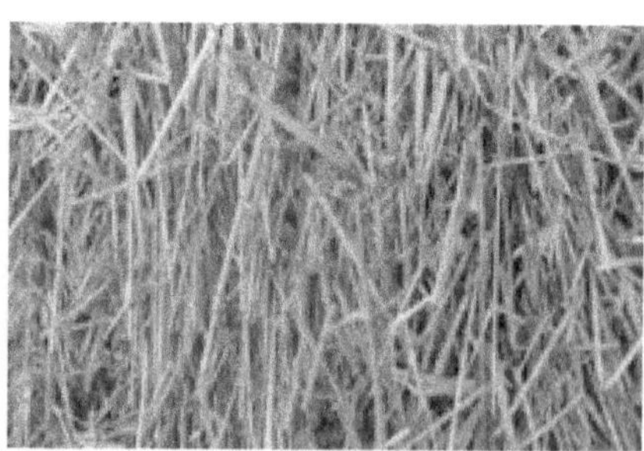

http://t2.gstatic.com/images?q=tbn:ANd9GcQj7_sAQwDBv61gDJEEDL7CRK84tvhl2qSyFb1Z4sgLeF7pH-AqN1d7CY8

If you decide to grow mushrooms from spores then you must sterilize the straw or other type of substrate you are intending to use. This is important as if you do not sterilize it then you will not know what else may already be in the substrate. The most effective way to do this is to place your straw or other substrate into a microwaveable bowl and add some water. All the straw should be damp. You can then place the bowl into the microwave for two or three minutes. This should be enough time for the water to boil off and the straw to be dry. In the process you will kill any bugs which may be on the substrate.

If you are intending to plant a lot of mushroom spores you may need to complete this part of the process in stages. If you do not kill off the microorganisms you may find that your mushrooms do not grow others ones grow in their place or that the mushrooms either do not taste right or make you ill.

This step only applies if you are growing from spores. If you have purchased spawn in a substrate then you cannot repeat this process as you will kill your mushrooms as well as any other bacteria. This process will have been completed by those supplying you with the spawn.

Tip 2

Whenever possible get the substrate right. Although most mushrooms will grow on a bed of straw, there are many which will grow much better if they are on their preferred substrate. This may be compost, rotten wood or even sawdust. A little research before you start the process will ensure that you have the best possible medium for planting. In turn this will ensure that you produce the tasty mush-rooms. It should also ensure that your substrate continues to produce mush-rooms for months and not simply for a few days or a week. The right substrate makes a huge difference to the quality and quantity of your mushrooms; regardless of which type they are.

The following should provide a guide as to the right substrate for your chosen mushroom;

http://previewcf.turbosquid.com/Preview/2015/09/28__15_09_51/thumbnail.png54fdfe07-297d-45b4-867e-c5d7612c1a95Original.jpg

Wood logs, particularly ones which are starting to rot are an excellent home for Shiitake, Oyster, Lion's Mane, Reishi and Maitake. You can cut your own logs by removing a short section from a hardwood tree. You must have a piece which is approximately two feet long and roughly four inches across its circumference. You will then need to keep the log somewhere for a couple of weeks, this will ensure it has died and started to decay. However, it is important to keep it moist during this period; you do not want the log to dry out as this will not provide a good environment for your spawn or spores.

To plant your spores you will need to drill several holes down the length of the log; they should be approximately six inches away from each other. You can then add a second row of holes parallel to the gaps spaces between the first row of holes. These should be two or three inches from the first holes and create a zigzag pattern. You can do this on one side or right the way around the log. You must then fill each hole with your spawn until it is level with the edge of the bark. You can then add melted cheese wax to the top of each hole; this will prevent unwanted microorganisms from getting in.

Compost or wood chips are excellent for White button mushrooms, Wine caps, Almond, Enoki and Shaggy Mane. As already mentioned it must be sterilized before you add the spores.

Tip 3

http://researchmatters.psu.edu/files/2016/02/Branched-Oyster-Mushroom-02.jpg

One of the most common questions is trying to work out when your mushrooms are ready to be picked and eaten. You will want to pick them when they are the best to provide maximum enjoyment and to allow the remaining spores to grow as well. The most obvious answer to this question is when the mushrooms look as you would expect them too. Part of familiarizing yourself with the mushrooms before you start growing them is to know what they will look like when they are grown. The other side of this is that you should only be growing mushrooms that you will enjoy eating. There is little point in growing them just for the sake of it. If you enjoy them then you should already know what they look like!

This is an important point as a mushroom which is ready can be simply twisted between your finger and thumb; it will almost fall off its stem. However, although this is a good way of knowing they are ripe it is not good for the young fungi still looking to grow and produce future mushrooms. Twisting and plucking is likely to reduce your overall harvest. It is therefore; best to pick them when they look ready. In general this will correspond with the time that the cap releases from the stem and before the spores are released.

Tip 4

It is possible to purchase a kit for growing mushrooms and this can be an excellent idea for anyone new to this. A grow kit does exactly as it suggests, provides all the essential parts for you to be able to grow your own mushrooms. A kit will usually include spawn as opposed to spawn and will have detailed instructions regarding how to look after the spawn and when to expect a harvest. Mushrooms generally grow much quicker from the spawn stage and require very little monitoring. This makes them an idea project to learn from and improve your knowledge ready to start the process from the very beginning the next time.

Obviously if you are purchasing a kit then you will be specifying which type of mushroom to have and this will not stop you from starting your own project from scratch as well.

Tip 5

Knowing your mushroom is critical! It is possible to make a mushroom fruit. This is when they get ready to release spores and are perfect for picking. Many types of mushroom can produce one or two lots of fruit and then seem to stagnate. This can be to do with an environmental issue such as too hot or too cold, but it can just as easily be something that you cannot identify and correct. This can be extremely frustrating when you have tried hard to produce a good mushroom and have even had some success.

By learning as much as you can about your mushrooms you may be able to force it to fruit and produce a fresh new crop. For instances, mushrooms which grow on logs can usually be forced by giving them a shock of water, instead of the usually damping. This is an extension of the fight or flight response that human's have. If you throw a bucket of cold water over the log, or even submerge the log for up to twenty four hours. This will help to convince the mushrooms that it is spring and time to produce a new batch of mushrooms.

Of course, when you submerge it you must weight it down or it will float and only some of the spores or spawn will respond. Wood can easily be weighted with a stone and watched for twenty four hours. You will know that the fruiting has been successful as tiny white buds will appear in the bark and gradually break through. These will then grow and transform into delicious mushrooms ripe for the picking! It is worth noting that it will take three or four years for the log to be covered in mushrooms. You should always let your log rest after you have completed a forced fruiting. Ideally it should rest for at least two months before, if needed you start the procedure again. If you do it too often the log will weaken and not be able to support the mushrooms. Equally it is believed that if you are prepared to wait you will get larger mushrooms as a result of your patience.

Chapter 3 – 10 Advanced Tips and Tricks for Successful Growing

Once you have managed to grow some mushrooms from either spores or spawn you will probably be looking to improve on your results the following year. There are a variety of ways in which you can enjoy even better results; the most obvious of these is by collecting your own spores and nurturing them to produce an even larger number of mushrooms.

Tip 1 - Collecting the Spores

https://i.ytimg.com/vi/UFgg8ZBLruY/maxresdefault.jpg

There are a variety of methods for collecting the spores from a mushroom and using them to grow new ones. Perhaps the simplest one is to start by making a spore print. This is a means by which you can identify the spores from a mushroom without needing to use a microscope; which is probably something you do not possess.

It is best to attempt this for the first time by purchasing some white button mush-rooms from a shop. Ideally you should be able to see the gills already. You will need two pieces of paper; one white and one black. You will also need a glass jar or similar container which can be placed over the mushroom; this will ensure the spores do not escape when you harvest them.

To start with you need to place both pieces of paper side by side and then remove the stem from your mushroom. Next, place the cap of the mushroom onto your paper; it needs to be spore side down and half on the black piece and half on the white. You then simply cover the mushroom with the glass jar and leave it overnight to allow the spores to drop out.

Because the paper is black and white the spores will be visible regardless of the shade. From this it is possible to print the spores and identify them. However for the purposes of planting it is simply a case of sprinkling them over a container which has been prepared with manure, compost or straw. You are then able to follow the procedures already described for nurturing and growing your mush-rooms.

Tip 2 – Oyster Mushrooms

http://botit.botany.wisc.edu/toms_fungi/images/post2.jpg

The easiest mushrooms to grow are oyster mushrooms; this means these are the best ones for any inexperienced mushroom grower to start with. They can be grown on fresh straw or hard wood. It is easiest to grow them in pasteurized straw; which can be achieved by following the guidelines in this book. These mushrooms can take up to a year before you see the first harvest but you can speed the growing process and avoid the need to pasteurize the growing medium by using coffee grounds after they have been through the machine.

Tip 3 – Spawn

The more spawn or spores you use the greater the chances of success when growing mushrooms. This is the same principle as in many other walks of life.

Tip 4 – Filter Patch grow Bags

These are specially designed bags which you can place your coffee grounds or over substrate into, along with the spores and they will be in the perfect growing environment as well as being better protected from other micro organisms or potential competitors. If you are unable to locate a filter bag you can create your own with a medium sized freezer bag, ice cream tub or even a milk carton. Simply clean it out thoroughly and add several small holes to the sides.

Tip 5 – Obtaining the medium for Free

If you plan to use coffee grounds as your growing medium then you will be able to pick up as much as you need by simply visiting your local coffee shop. The majority of coffee shops will get through loads of coffee grounds in one day and will be happy to pass some onto you. This will be free! You should ensure the coffee waste you get is fresh, i.e. less than twenty four hours old. You can then get if straight home and plant your spores of spawn. For the best results you should mix your spores with the coffee in a bowl and then seal it up tight. You can then simply place the entire contents into your filter bag and wait for them to grow.

Tip 6 – Growing magic Mushrooms

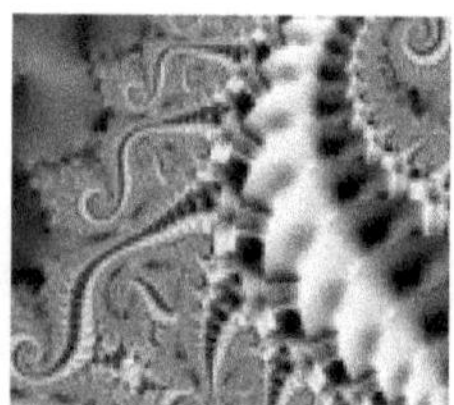

http://static5.businessinsider.com/image/545bcdca6bb3f72c0777a969-480/psychedelia.jpg

In the past this has been said to be extremely difficult for a beginner to achieve. However, thanks to rapidly improving ideas and techniques it is now possible to grow the magic mushroom at home!

As with any mushroom growing techniques it is essential to sterilize the equipment and the growing medium before adding the spores to the container. The spores and substrate need to be an area of high humidity for the first three weeks. This type of environment must be sustained when the substrate is removed from its sterile environment and added to a more mundane place, such as an old fish tank. The substrate should now be filled with spawn; this will make it extremely difficult for any other microorganisms to infiltrate or affect the growing mushrooms. The environment must remain extremely humid. You should start to see mature mushrooms ready for use within a few weeks. At this point it is likely that you will have more than you need. You can dry excess mushrooms and store them for several months.

Tip 7 - Time or Money

It is a wonderful experience producing your own mushrooms from scratch. However, it can be time consuming to collect the spores, add them to the right substrate and nurse them through their first few weeks of life. Although purchasing the spawn ready to be planted is a more expensive option you may find that this is a better application of the time you have available and you will still have the satisfaction of producing your own mushrooms with the added benefit of them being available quicker.

Tip 8 – Survival Food

Whilst most people may not think of survival whilst growing their mushrooms it is an important part of society and a subject which is becoming increasingly popular. If something were top happen which changed the face of the earth then you may need to quickly learn how to grow as many different things as possible. Mushrooms are not only exceptionally easy to grow they are full of a wide array of nutrients and vitamins which can help to provide you with a balanced diet.

Tip 9 – Dried

https://thecandidadiaries.files.wordpress.com/2012/11/dried-shiitakes.jpg

Another excellent reason for growing mushrooms is the lack of wastage. Once the mushroom has finally grown you may quickly find you are overwhelmed by the sheer quantity of them. Whilst they will always taste best fresh they can be an excellent choice when dried. This process will also allow you to keep the mushroom for a much longer period and use them when necessary.

Tip 10 – Hydrated Lime

An alternative to cooking your straw in the microwave to sterilize your substrate is to use lime instead. You do not need to be exact for this method. Simply add a large handful of lime to a barrel of water and soak your straw. It will need to be weighted to ensure it cannot float. The straw needs to stay submerged for approximately eighteen hours.

You can then drain the excess water and the straw is damp and ready for use.

Conclusion

Growing mushrooms is a lot of fun, it is also an excellent way to use some spare space and create a delicious addition to virtually any meal. It is also a useful skill to develop should a disaster ever occur and you are left to survive on your own. Many mushrooms are extremely high in vitamins and minerals which will help you function properly.

There are a variety of methods which can be used to grow your own mushrooms, these range from the simple; such as purchasing spawn which is already starting to grow. You can also harvest your own spores and grow the mushrooms from nothing. This process is longer but allows you more control over each step.

Growing mushrooms is not a new thing but it is more difficult than many people realize. The result can often be very disappointing. However, by following the steps in this book and utilizing the tips provided you are almost guaranteed to be successful. It is advisable to start with either white button mushrooms or oyster mushrooms as these are the easiest to grow. You will then be able to graduate to other types of mushrooms as your technique, knowledge and growing methods improve. Perhaps the most important thing to remember is that mushrooms need very little light to grow. They are happiest in a cool dark place with plenty of humidity; this replicates their environment in the wild and will provide you with the best chance of successfully creating your own delicious mushrooms.

Mushroom growing is becoming increasingly popular and this means there is a far greater array of information available as well as social media groups and potentially even local groups who will meet to discuss techniques, provide advice and even swap tips. These groups can be a valuable source of additional information and help you to successful grow your own mushrooms. Providing you stick to the rules in this book there is no reason why you will not have success growing mushrooms at home. The better you get at growing mushrooms the more advanced techniques you will be able to try as you understand the factors involved and why each step is so important. It is true to say that each step must be completed properly all the mushrooms are unlikely to grow.

FREE Bonus Reminder

If you have not grabbed it yet, please go ahead and download your special bonus E book *"Chakras for Beginners. 7 Steps To Understand And Balance Chakras, Radiate Energy, And Strengthen Aura".*

Simply Click the Button Below

OR Go to This Page

http://lifehacksworld.com/free

BONUS #2: More Free & Discounted Books & Products

Do you want to receive more Free/Discounted Books or Products?

We have a mailing list where we send out our new Books or Products when they go free or with a discount on Amazon. Click on the link below to sign up for Free & Discount Book & Product Promotions.

=> Sign Up for Free & Discount Book & Product Promotions <=

OR Go to this URL

http://zbit.ly/1WBb1Ek